A STUDY OF NATIVE AMERICAN SINGING AND SONG

A STUDY OF NATIVE AMERICAN SINGING AND SONG

William J. Lavonis

Native American Studies
Volume 16

The Edwin Mellen Press
Lewiston•Queenston•Lampeter

Library of Congress Cataloging-in-Publication Data

Lavonis, William J.
   A study of Native American singing and song / William J. Lavonis.
      p. cm. -- (Native American studies ; v. 16)
   Includes bibliographical references and index.
   ISBN: 978-0-7734-0865-4
   1. Tewa Indians--Music--History and criticism. 2. Indians of North
America--Music--History and criticism. 3. Singing. I. Title. II. Series.

ML3557.L34 2005
782.42162'97494--dc22

2004060976

This is volume 16 in the continuing series
Native American Studies
Volume 16
NAS Series ISBN 0-88946-482-0

A CIP catalog record for this book is available from the British Library

Front cover: Taos Pueblo, summer 2001, taken by author

Copyright © 2004   William J. Lavonis

All rights reserved. For information contact

        The Edwin Mellen Press   The Edwin Mellen Press
             Box 450   Box 67
         Lewiston, New York   Queenston, Ontario
         USA 14092-0450   CANADA L0S 1L0

The Edwin Mellen Press, Ltd.
Lampeter, Ceredigion, Wales
UNITED KINGDOM SA48 8LT

Printed in the United States of America

**LOVINGLY DEDICATED TO MY PARENTS,
ROSE AND BILL LAVONIS**

CONTENTS

Acknowledgements		i
Foreword – Dr. Sharon A. Hansen		iii
Introduction - William J. Lavonis		v
1.	Peter Garcia and San Juan Pueblo	1
2.	Native Vocal Pedagogy	15
3.	The Making of Native Songs	23
	Accompaniment	
	Native Singers	
	Some Historic Native Singers of Note	
4.	Western Composers and Native Songs	37
Appendices:		
	A. Song Collectors and Ethnologists	49
	B. Pueblo Contact Information	50
	C. Selected Native Websites	51
	D. Selected Recordings from San Juan Pueblo	51
Bibliography		53
Index		58

ACKNOWLEDGEMENTS

I would like to thank The Museum of New Mexico in Santa Fe and their library staff for all of their marvelous help in locating out of print articles and books relating to Native American singing, my colleagues Sharon Hansen for her keen eye in editing and Christopher Peterson for his computer expertise, Dr. Richard Sjoerdsma, editor of the NATS Journal of Singing, Peter Garcia for his open and giving nature, and my partner, Kurt Ollmann for his unflagging support.

William Lavonis
University of Wisconsin-Milwaukee
July 2004

FOREWORD

By

Sharon A. Hansen

DMA, University of Wisconsin-Milwaukee

For the Native American, singing is a primary means of communicating with the sacred Holy Beings. It is a way of imparting tradition through the generations. It is seldom performed for its own sake, serving instead a central role in the activities of daily life. It is regarded as one of the most sacred of traditions of the people: indeed, in Navajo, the name for *singer* is also the name for *healer/medicine person*.[1] Dr. Charlotte Heth, Assistant Director for Public Programs at the National Museum of the American Indian, writes, "The importance of American Indian music is found… in the traditions and values it expresses to and for the Indian people. This oral tradition has survived solely because the music was too important to be allowed to die."[2]

Dr. William Lavonis, Professor of Voice and Opera Studies at the University of Wisconsin – Milwaukee, has undertaken a labor of love in his investigation of Native American Singing and Song. His interview with San Juan Pueblo singer Peter Garcia is at once deeply poignant and refreshingly sincere, offering a vivid definition of Mr. Garcia's profound words, *"You pray double when you sing."* Dr. Lavonis' description of native vocal pedagogy will be of interest to all those who teach and perform music outside the narrow confines of the Euro-Romantic operatic tradition. His commentary on the making of native songs accentuates similarities and differences between native and non-native song composition, transmission, and performance. Finally, his discussion of the use of native songs by western composers, as well as the additional useful information

---

[1] Arlie Neskahi, Rainbow Walker Music, accessed July 1, 2004,
<http://p217.ezboard.com/furban4estfrm10.showMessage?topicID=4.topic>
[2] Heth, Charlotte. Liner notes for audio recording "Songs of Earth, Water, Fire and Sky." New World Records #80246 – 2.

found in four appendices, all lead the reader to an enlightened respect and appreciation for Native American singing and song traditions.

Alfonso Ortiz (1939-1998), born at the San Juan Pueblo, was one of the most prolific native scholars of his generation. Professor of Anthropology at Princeton and Rutgers Universities, he returned home to end his career at his alma mater, the University of New Mexico. This short introduction ends with Dr. Ortiz' translation of verses from "Oku Shareh," Pueblo Turtle Dance Songs of the San Juan Pueblo, mentioned in the Lavonis-Garcia interview. The words compel the reader onward, to hear the singing voice of these holy people:

> Over in the direction where the sun descends,
> Deep, deep within the sacred lake,
> From there the joyous singing
> Of holy people comes forth!
>
> Hapembe! Hapembe! Hapembe!
>
> Holy people are now emerging!
> Holy people are now coming!
> Holy people, with their singing and calling,
> Have arrived here! [3]

---

[3] Translation copyright 1979, Alfonso Ortiz, New World Records.

INTRODUCTION

By

William J. Lavonis

"You pray double when you sing" was one of the first statements made to me by Peter Garcia of San Juan Pueblo when I interviewed him for the contents of this book. The research is the result my yearlong sabbatical in Santa Fe, NM, which was granted me by the University of Wisconsin-Milwaukee during the 2000-2001 school year. Its purpose is to foster an appreciation for Native American singing and songs, as well as include in one place some of the pedagogical mysteries of the vocal art of the Native American. Because of the large number of tribes and traditions in Native North America, this study will focus on those vocal practices which have been referred to by ethnomusicologists in previously published information and on the pueblo villages near Santa Fe where I was able to observe ceremonial singing firsthand. Chapter 1 consists of my experiences with San Juan Pueblo singer, Peter Garcia; Chapter 2 delves into Native voice pedagogy; Chapter 3 describes the composition and performance of Native songs and their singers; and Chapter 4 presents a listing of Western and Native composers and their vocal works based on Native American melodies.

PETER GARCIA AND SAN JUAN PUEBLO

San Juan Pueblo is located twenty-five miles northeast of Santa Fe near Española on Highway 68--- the road to Taos. The largest *Tewa* speaking pueblo, it is known as *Ohkay Owingeh* meaning "Village of the Strong People." The Spaniards declared it the first capital of New Mexico in 1598, and like many of the pueblos it has managed to combine its traditions successfully with the Catholic/Hispanic culture. June 24 is the village feast day honoring St. John the Baptist.

The Garcia Family of San Juan boasts generations of singers who have performed at colleges and museums throughout the United States, Spain and Santa Fe, including the National Museum of American History and the Smithsonian Festival of American Folklife. They have been recorded by such labels as Music of the World, Smithsonian, and New World Records. Peter Garcia, also known in *Tewa* as *Kwa-Phade* or "Passing Rain," has taken on his father's *Tewa* song legacy. Coming from a family of twelve boys, Peter was born in 1927 at San Juan and served for four years in the Navy during World War II's South Pacific Theater. While serving the United States, he heeded the Spirits' call to return to San Juan and rediscover his musical roots.

At Peter's invitation I attended the *Tembishare* or Harvest Dance at San Juan Pueblo on September 23, 2000. When I arrived at the village early that Saturday morning, Natives from other Pueblos were quietly setting up tables to sell jewelry, loaves of bread, and slices of prune pie. In the Native Arts and Crafts Cooperative I was told by the proprietor, Pauline, that the dance used to take place every four years but now occurs annually and on a weekend to accommodate those Natives who have jobs off the reservation. While I browsed at the Native American crafts and pottery, I experienced a clash of cultures when the radio tuned to the local fine arts station began playing a symphony by Samuel Barber!

As I entered the plaza surrounded by small adobe dwellings, I smelled a strong aroma of fresh fruit. In the open area near where the Harvest Dance would take place, I saw a pile of crushed apples, watermelons, muskmelons, and squash. As Indians arrived, they approached the mound, smashed a melon or other harvest fruit in the center, uttered a blessing, and then tossed a handful of cornmeal over their offering.

Throughout the day one could hear intermingling of English with the *Tewa* language as young and old made their way to the dance site. Many brought their own lawn chairs and set them up under a lone locust tree to shield themselves from the sun. The older women wore colorful wraps, as the wind was quite brisk. Free-running dogs were everywhere and squeals of delight came from children, perhaps in anticipation of gifts they might receive from the harvest dancers.

Around 11 a.m., approximately 130 dancers and eight male singers entered the plaza, led by six *koshares* (clowns) painted with grey and white stripes on their torsos, arms, and legs and concentric circles on their faces. They wore headdresses of two limp horns decorated with cornhusks, reminiscent of a jester's hat. The women were dressed in black skirts, colorful shawls and white shin-length moccasins. They wore flowers or feathers in their hair as did the men, who wore dark pants and colorful shirts. After circling the plaza once, the dancers, who had been carrying baskets, bags, and satchels, stopped moving and began pelting the eager spectators with produce, household items, toys, candy, small pieces of jewelry. During the singing, the *koshares* called out in high voices with pointed, laughing-like calls. The strong, forceful beat of Peter Garcia's drum led his singers through nearly one hour of constant singing, mesmerizing the observers with his strong, clear sound and infecting his singing partners with his high standards of textual clarity and good vocal technique. They sang in the baritone range with darkened vowels, obvious intercostal breathing, loose jaws, and relaxed faces with their heads and necks in perfect alignment. The male dancers joined in the singing while the women dancers and Native spectators mouthed the words, leaving no one present as a passive observer. As the configuration of the dancers changed and the circle moved, many dancers greeted friends and relatives as they passed by them.

About a half-hour into the ceremony, one of the dancers spotted two Anglo men photographing the event. The Pueblo police were summoned and the violators had their film confiscated and were asked to leave the premises, as photos of the ceremony were not permitted that day. After the dance, the crowd approached the mound of sweet scented crushed melons and fruit, helping themselves to refreshment in honor of the harvest. As Peter Garcia had said during one interview in 1992, "As long as they have their songs and dances, the San Juan people participate in an endlessly renewable dawn." [1]

The following interview with Peter took place on September 18, 2000. Imagine a large, jovial man, given to bursts of laughter and infectious good humor.

BL: What I am really interested in most of all, along with the traditions, is the vocal technique--the way that you use the language and the way you use your bodies in order to produce sound.
PG: You might need a little background of what I really am. When I was growing up here, our language was nothing but *Tewa*. That was our main communication. I didn't learn any English until I attended the elementary school here when I was about seven years old. I still speak fluent *Tewa*. My songs are related to what I was taught by the Elders and I try to make them more [accessible] to people that are nonspeakers. In my heart and in my mind, I said, what's the use of composing songs if you can't make the nonspeakers understand?
BL: When did you learn how to sing?

---

[4] Peter Garcia, "Perspectives of a Contemporary Tewa Composer" *Musical Repercussions of 1492*; (Washington, D.C.: Smithsonian Institution 1992): 93-96.

PG: I learned how to sing [when] we were taking part in the dances. You had to learn the songs, to do the sudden steps, the sudden movements included with the song. Those things stuck with me--the motions, the rhythm and everything.

BL: Did you find anything about that difficult?

PG: Well, you know, it came automatic because [if] you listen and you are a good listener, you become a good communicator and those songs will be easy for you to handle.

BL: Are there people who don't do well?

PG: Well, you know, it's like anything else. There are slow learners and there are mediocre and there are talented ones. I caught on to [the songs] as I grew. As I got educated and I learned the English language, [I realized] that the Elders didn't [always understand what they sang]. They knew that that word was there, but what [did] it mean? We were mentioning the day and night, the colors, the directions, Mother Earth. We needed to express and interpret what we said in *Tewa* to the nonspeakers. It came to my mind [when] I finally joined the Navy and I spent four years there that the Spirits were calling me: you have to get back to your community--to your village.

BL: When you compose your songs, do you write them down?

PG: No.

BL: So it's strictly all in the mind?

PG: All in the mind! And they have to come from the heart! I asked the Spirits to come help me and I think, by golly, they *do*! When I came back from the service in '50, I began to get into the middle of the head-singers and from there on I climbed up. Now, that's what I am--a head-singer. I [try] to encourage younger generations--mainly my sons, because most of the song singing is done by male voices. And the drumming and even the songs are created by men. There's a lot of rituals that are involved in it. People don't realize, it's not just you say-- "we're going to do a dance." You have to make a lot of preparation--especially in those big traditional dances.

BL: How many songs have you composed?

PG: Ohhhhh, *many*, many songs.

BL: Hundreds, maybe?

PG: Yeah. I wish I had written them down. Since 1955, right along in that area, I had already composed many of the songs--the Buffalo Dance song, the Eagle Dance song, the Butterfly Dance song. Some of those I have a group of my grandchildren perform. I go to the schools and try to make recordings and teach them the simple ones.

BL: And your main instrument is drum.

PG: Yeah, my main "guitar" is the drum.

BL: Got it! Do you play any others?

PG: We have the rattle. Those are the main instruments of the traditional dance songs.

BL: So when you're getting ready to do a dance, what do you do in preparation for the ceremony?

PG: It first comes from the War Chief of the tribe and whatever is agreed on to perform the particular dance. They let me know and then they have another meeting. So while we're there, we decide to create the songs for that particular dance. During the Christmas holidays, the Turtle Dance is the main dance and traditionally it has been handed down from generation to generation. Every 26 of December [the] Turtle Dance is performed. We set a date for all men who will be participating in this particular dance to get together in the War Chief's home (the president) and then we expose the songs that we have created. Mostly it's just done by me. So I just sing it out to them, and then if somebody else has one, I listen to it. You become like a critic.

BL: So you make some changes?

PG: Yeah, a few changes so we'll all feel comfortable. There's four songs. That's where the directions come in: North, West, South, East. I call them the elements. And there's a lot of spiritual beings that are mentioned-- the *Kachina*, and then the tribal people. I base my songs on the events of the whole year. You know, we have farming, the crops that we raised, the corn, the wheat, directions. I finally found out as I went on that the directions and the colors are related. In the *Tewa* area I learned that the North is blue, and then the West is yellow, then to the South is red, and to the East is white. Those songs have to have a melody where they'll fit in. You don't want to go way up and you don't want to go way too low. After we compose the songs and we got it plain and simple and we feel comfortable, we come to the *kivas* [sacred ceremonial chamber] and there's more participation. They learn from listening and then they sing out, too.

BL: Do you ever sing real high?

PG: Sometimes I do, but I try not to. . .

BL: Because you really want the participation of everyone.

PG: Right.

BL: That's very much like our Christian churches that want the whole congregation to sing together rather than just have one person up there singing.

PG: Yeah, well, I sing in church. I belong to a choir called Trilingual and they play the instruments--the accordion and the guitar. I'm their main voice because I can sing tenor-high. I can go up there and then I can come down to bass.

BL: So you have a pretty big range.

PG: Uh, huh. And then my voice is so loud and clear that they say, " You don't need a microphone."

BL: So they do sing with some amplification?

PG: Oh, yeah.

BL: Do you ever do that in the dances?

PG: No, not in the dances. It's way different.

BL: You just have to learn to project your voice so that people can hear in a larger situation like that.

PG: Yeah. Some of them come to me like you and say, "We want to hear you because your voice is explicit--it explains. We watch your lips and those words." Well, again, going back to the Elders--some of the words that they were using, they kind of mumble-like. And I [asked myself] what is the meaning of *that*?

What wants to be said? I want to be sure that what I'm singing is clear enough so that I can explain to the nonspeaker.

BL: How do you explain the *vocables* [wordless sounds] that occur? I know that in classical music there are times, say, in opera where you will be singing on one long vowel--/a/, /i/ or /u/-- [International Phonetic Alphabet] in the middle of a song.

PG: I know what you mean. [*Vocables*] are included in some of the songs like [in] the beginnings. Let me give you an example of the Turtle Dance. There's "/a/, /a/, /a/, /a/, /Ei/, /Ei/, /Ei/, /Ei/." That's the formula--the beginning--but in the middle section you have wording and then you say "/a/, /wi/, /aja/" and that doesn't mean anything--its just a resting point for you so you feel comfortable.

BL: Is it also a resting point for your mind to recall what your next verse is maybe? Or is it strictly a resting point for your body or your voice?

PG: I think it's both.

BL: Do you have anything to keep yourself healthy vocally?

PG: I sing out! I sing everyday!

BL: Do you ever lose your voice?

PG: No, I haven't, surprisingly.

BL: Do you feel tired after singing an entire dance?

PG: Oh yeah! I'm just a human being. I get tired. The practices have a lot to do--

BL: With building up your stamina?

PG: Yeah. I think that's what helps me not to lose my voice.

BL: Just like exercise.

PG: Yeah. Exercising my vocal cords and everything else (I do a lot of beating of the drums). Right now we are preparing for the Harvest Dance. We're gonna perform on Saturday, the twenty-third here and I am beating the drum. We have society leaders and the songs are related to that. Each leader has its own song. And they're so different! And there's eleven of them--one right after another. We had our first session last night.

BL: Do you have any special remedy if you have a sore throat or sickness? Is there anything that you've heard that Native singers do?

PG: Well, they have some herbs. They call it in *Tewa "Osa'puh."* It's a sort of like bitter root that they chew and they swallow some of the juice from that.

BL: Is it something that grows around here?

PG: Well, I don't know. I think it's something that grows in the mountains. In Spanish they call it *Osha*. So far, thank God--thank the Spirits-- I'm there to sing out. Sure, if I sing one whole day, maybe the following day I wouldn't sing as well as I sang yesterday, but I can still sing out.

BL: Have you found that your voice has changed since you were a young person? Are there things that are easier or more difficult to do with your voice?

PG: I think they're easier now because I am more familiar with the formula. But in the past, when I was just a young guy like you guys, I had to think twice.

BL: What is your concept of how you breathe when you sing? In voice teaching we talk about expanding your ribs and breathing deep down into your abdomen. Do you have a sensation that you do that or is it subconscious?

PG: Well, [it comes] automatic now. It was hard in the past when I was younger and I think that has to do with you are afraid to sing out. I feel comfortable with every song that I sing.

BL: Where do you feel your voice vibrate in your body?

PG: I think it's coming from the mouth and lips and here and here [pointing to his chest].

BL: So you are like a total vibrating body in a way.

PG: Yeah, I think so.

BL: Do you ever have to sing softly?

PG: Yeah, sometimes I do.

BL: In the opera world when they're practicing the final rehearsals before opening the show, they allow the singers to do what they call "marking" --to sing softly so that they save their energy for the performance the next day. Is there anything like that in your rehearsals?

PG: It's just full out all the time. I tell them, "You sing out. You're inside practicing, tomorrow you go out in the open and you're gonna sing out and let's get used to it."

BL: To build up stamina.

PG: Yeah, build up, exactly. There is no way of trying to save your voices for the final performance. I feel more comfortable when I sing out loud. That way I'm sure I'm gonna do the same thing out there. They like the way we sing here. The dancers know when to stop and when to go with the drumbeats. I tell them, "the heartbeat of that drum, it's like it's telling you 'this is how it goes.' Listen to it."

BL: Do you feel like you get the tempo of a song from your own body rhythm, your own heartbeat?

PG: Yeah, because when I'm creating songs, I usually use myself as a model: if I do this at this speed, the other dancers will feel the same way--not too fast--just where you feel comfortable.

BL: In learning how to sing high, was it from imitating what you had heard from other singers or imitating animal sounds? Or is it just a matter of trying to project?

PG: No, I think it's just a matter of projection. You have to use your own judgment, too. How would I sound to the listeners? If I go too high and the other singers don't feel comfortable, I can tell. And in the movement of the dancers, too. I can tell if I'm drumming too fast, and I come back down and they change.

BL: Do you feel like it's easier to sing when you're standing up, sitting, or moving around and dancing?

PG: I think standing.

BL: Because you could probably get a good intake of air and feel like you're using the whole body. Not moving around?

PG: Maybe just a slight motion--not too much.

BL: Have you ever been moved to tears while you're singing or to laughter?

PG: No, I don't think so--to laughter probably, because maybe somebody that you know is out there in the audience and you feel happy that he's there.

BL: Never crying?

PG: No, never crying.

BL: Have you experienced nerves and fear?

PG: Yeah, fear.

BL: And what does that do to your voice?

PG: I don't know whether it shows or it even appears to anybody that I'm in fear. Just to myself.

BL: Do you feel that you get short of breath, if you're fearful?

PG: Yeah, right.

BL: What do you like about your own voice?

PG: I think that my voice has a lot of strength. I know from the heart that what I am singing is pronounced right, clear, so that other people can understand it. I feel great about singing.

BL: How would you teach a young one to sing?

PG: I would teach him to listen carefully first before. In the *Tewa* world the songs that are sung are put into motion and they need to learn the songs and feel comfortable so they can do the certain steps from the drumbeat. I tell them, "You listen clearly, that's where your listening skills come in. The steps will come later."

BL: So the steps are the last thing?

PG: Well, not really the last thing.

BL: Rhythm first?

PG: Yeah, rhythm first, then the drumbeats, then the wordings of the song. Usually in the *Tewa* world you begin your dance on your right foot. We still do the *Matachines* here at San Juan and I performed that since I was a teenager. It is done with a violin and a guitar and it's part of a dance that was brought to San Juan here by Oñate and performed during the Christian holidays, so it was related to the birth of Christ. The Indian people from San Juan learned it. They still put that into the Turtle Dance. Those are a combination because it is a three-day celebration here in San Juan and it's still going--still being handed down. On December twenty-fourth and twenty-fifth, the *Matachines*, and the evening of

Christmas Eve we perform the Sunset Dance in preparation for the Turtle Dance on the twenty-sixth. Anyway going back to the steps we use in the Indian dances, we always use our right foot first. My dad was a composer of songs and he asked me, "Which foot do you begin all your Indian dances?" And I says, "the right." He said, "No, whether you know it or not (you've been dancing all these years) in the *Matachines* you begin with your left foot, because it's a non-traditional dance." He woke me up! It makes a lot of sense that the non-Indian people and the Tewa, even though they were struggling and fighting with each other, they became friends and created the *Matachines* [which is] related to the Turtle Dance for the Christmas holidays.

BL: It put the two cultures together. Are there any other musical styles that interest you outside of your Native music?

PG: Well, I like to hear tunes like Westerns. That was kind of popular when I was going to school in the 40s. Who used to be the singers? Roy Acuff, Hank Williams. I liked them. And then I like church music. I learned the church hymns when they were in Latin. In 1964, they changed to English liturgy and it became more interesting--then they changed it to Spanish and it's still being done. They have a church in each pueblo and a saint and feast day for that particular saint. I sing "How Great thou Art" and "Amazing Grace" in *Tewa*. I learned it by heart. The other ones—oh, the hard-metal music! --it's just not for me. Just like (not to be critical) but the Native American singers of the Plains Indian in your area--they sing out like they're gonna bust their vocal cords [demonstrates in a high, belting falsetto]. I don't feel comfortable. I think you're tiring yourself.

BL: Your approach is a little more mellow. Would you read a *Tewa* poem for me?

PG: You know, I can speak the *Tewa* language real fluently, but when it comes to reading it's just Greek. There's so many sounds. [And] when it comes to writing--it's hard! You wanna hear the drum?

BL: I'd love it! Now, where did you get your drum?

PG: This one was made over in Taos. I have a son-in-law in Taos. His brother is a drum-maker. When I was teaching in Española Valley in the early 70s, the students gave me a drum, and during that summer I left it out here and when my daughter came, she didn't see it. She ran over it! "We owe you a drum!" The following week, they brought me this one. This one is light. I've traveled with it for quite a while. This is the way the Cloud Dance goes . . . . (Sings)

BL: Great! Can you give a translation?

PG: In the bluish summer lake the (we call them *Koshares,* or the clowns) are dancing on top of that lake. They're preparing to bring the *Kachinas*. (The chorus starts:) They saw the *Kachinas* over at the lake at the Laguna Pueblo. They emerged bringing their corn here, to the pueblo--the blue corn, the yellow corn. There's five verses, but I just did three. It continues until the end with that loud beat of the drum. That's the cue for the singers and the [dancers] that the ending is coming. You probably heard the middle portion--the *hapimbe*. That is always connected to Native American Songs in the *Tewa* World--the *hapimbe*. Most of it is vocal. In the next verse they are bringing the moisture--the rain and the mist.

BL: What is the word for rain?

PG: *Kwa*--the falling of the rain--the water, moisture.

BL: Is this a traditional song or one that you composed?

PG: My dad composed that one way back when I was just a kid, but I put those words with it. We recorded [it]. My brother was a helper. We both composed songs, but he died in 1995.

BL: Did you have more than one brother?

PG: Yeah, there were twelve boys in the family. Nothing but boys. . .

BL: No kidding!

PG: No girls at all. But very few of us were singers and dancers. The others didn't really care.

BL: Does everyone embrace Christianity in the pueblo?

PG: [There is] pretty solid cooperation and support for the church here in the pueblo, [but] lately a few of them are shying away. They probably don't go, because I think they are depending more on the Indian ways and Indian style. I go for that, too.

BL: If I were to write an article for a singing teacher's magazine, would you have any objection to that? It is nonprofit; I don't make any money off of it. It's strictly for. . .

PG: For what you learned.

BL: Exactly.

PG: No, there's no objections, because I think a lot of these people want to find out what I do. It's a learning thing for people who want to advance more. The learners can find write-ups in the library, but unless you speak to a knowledgeable person like. . .

BL: Like you!

PG: Yeah, really! . . .there's not much cooperation. If an experienced person is asked about his knowledge, I think it's right that he should give permission and let somebody else study. That's the way I feel. I'm not taking these things with me. If I go, they go with me. If it's passed on to somebody, I will feel comfortable that I have left something on this earth for somebody. The Creator said share your knowledge with others.

Postscript: On June 7, 2001, at the Pojoaque Pueblo gift shop, I purchased Peter Garcia's latest CD, **Songs of My People** *and learned that Peter had passed away that morning from complications of liver cancer, nine months after our conversation.*

NATIVE VOICE PEDAGOGY

That there exists a pedagogy of Native American singing is evident in a study by William K. Powers entitled "*Ogalala* Song Terminology." Powers assembled the following list of *Ogalala* terms describing vocal qualities. "*Ya*" refers to the mouth and "*ho*" means "voice" in the language of this Teton Dakota tribe.

Describing tone:
    to growl as one sings--*yabu*
    to whine--*hokapsanpsan*
Dynamic level:
    to trail the voice--*yaiyowaza*
    to sing out--*hotun*
    loud voiced--*hotanka*
Special techniques:
    to make the voice rattle--*yahla*
    to sing slowly,drawl--*yazilya*
    to hum--*yahmun*
Vocal Health:
    to become hoarse from singing--*yahogita*
    to tire the voice from singing--*hoiyohpeya* [5]

In the Native American culture singing is taught through a trial and error method based mainly on imitation. Singing does not "come from the mouth but

---

[5] William K. Powers, "Ogalala Song Terminology," *Selected Reports in Ethnomusicology* 3, no. 2: 23-41

from somewhere in the singer's body," [6] a statement with which many Western pedagogues would agree, even though they might characterize Native vocal production as "hyperfunctional," "tense," "down in the throat," and "sobbing" in quality. Nonetheless, the male singers have the ability to create a powerful resonance, using open vowel sounds for projection, while the women tend to make a sound that, although thinner, also is capable of projection (witness the ululations or wordless high cries of the Cheyenne tribe). This loud dynamic is important for projection in an outdoor setting. Furthermore some tribes believe loud singing is necessary to make contact with distant spirits.[7] The average vocal compass of Native singers is greater than that of average non-natives because of the vast amount of singing they do in their lives. The men, who are mainly baritones and basses, have ranges of up to two octaves and can sing up to Cs without resorting to falsetto.[8] In addition, Natives tend to possess marvelous pitch memory and can consistently begin a song in the same key.

Native American song texts are interwoven with nonword syllables known as *vocables*, the origins of which will be discussed in detail in Chapter 3. The order of frequency in the use of the *vocable*/vowel sounds is /a/--1, /e/E/--2, /o/--3, /i/--4, /u/--rarely,[9] displaying the Native's preference for open sounds. Just as a classically trained singer gravitates to certain phonemes on which to vocalize, a Native singer may choose the vowel, that feels best in his voice. The use of the initial /h/ in many *vocables* is a way to begin the air stream and directly set the vocal folds vibrating. Further, the frequent use of the glides /j/ and /w/, and the liquid /l/ along with the predominance of open vowel sounds and a natural avoidance of the closed vowels, promotes freedom in the tongue and throat, encouraging unhampered air flow and allowing for maximum resonance. It would

---

[6] John Bierhorst, *A Cry from the Earth, Music of the North American Indians* (Santa Fe: Ancient City Press, 1979).
[7] Nora Yeh, "The Pogonshare Ceremony of the Tewa, San Juan, NM." *Selected Reports in Ethnomusicology*; 3, no. 2 101-145:121
[8] Thurlow Lieurance, "The Musical Soul of the American Indian." *The Etude* 655 (October 1920).
[9] Danita Ross, "Musical Mission: Taos studio keeps tribal songs on the record." *New Mexico Magazine* 70, no. 8 (1992): 39-44.

seem that many tried and tested pedagogical devices used in Western teaching methods developed independently in Native American pedagogy.

In the New Mexican Pueblo culture the singing style is mellower and generally employs a lower range than the vibrant, exciting style of the Great Plains tribes, which many non-natives call to mind as "Indian" music. The musical language is an amalgamation of three distinct traditions: Native American, Hispanic, and Western European. The Pueblo languages (*Tiwa*, *Tewa*, *Towa*, *Zuni*, and *Keres*) contain the five European vowel sounds /i/,/e/, /a/,/o/,/u/ plus /ae/ and /ɔ̄/ and a variety of harsh or soft nasal sounds, which vary among the 8 tribes. There are also frequent glottal stops between double vowel sounds and before initial ones, usually indicated by an apostrophe, as in the words "*O'ke 'anyu*" (San Juan girls).

In the Pueblos there are singing families who pass on traditions from one generation to the next, but singing is not closed to others wishing to learn. Each village has a distinct style ranging from solemn and restrained to lively and showy.[10] Tones range from fullthroated, soaring sounds to low, growl-like tones with rare use of falsetto. The throat is open, and heavy accents are employed, but the overall effect is relaxed. In my interview with San Juan Native Peter Garcia, I noted that he breathed through his nose and mouth and that his tongue position was forward in the Spanish/Italian manner.

Other observations from video recordings at the Museum of New Mexico showed the Pueblo Native's use of imperceptible breathing, a relaxed jaw, a small mouth opening with little lip motion, resulting in a sing-as-you-speak style with little neck tension and a legato line, despite what might be a rhythmically energetic song. There was some nasality present in speaking and singing and in one unusual case much neck and laryngeal movement coupled with shallow breathing.

---

[10] Gertrude Kurath, *Music and Dance of the Tewa Pueblos*. (Santa Fe: Museum of New Mexico Press, 1970).

In his observation of the *Zuni* tribe in Arizona and New Mexico, composer/song collector Carlos Troyer states that

" . . . Indians in general possess large lungs and are *deep* and *slow* breathers . . . " due in part to the high altitude. He further describes "a curious physiological condition prevails among these cliff-dwellers, which is not known to exist with other tribes, in that the structure of the hyoid bones of the tongue are found to extend in an outward and posterior position, whereby the vocal ligaments are enlarged and widened fully a third of an inch. Owing to this peculiarity men and women can equally affect a high tone of voice like that of a high soprano, or go to the other extreme of a basso profundo."[11]

Although they are from the same culture area and share many vocal traits with their Pueblo brothers, the Navajo Indians sing vigorously with a piercing high tone and with frequent breaks into falsetto.[12] Falsetto is used exclusively by these singers in the *Yeibichai* Dance or Winter Curing ceremony.[13] Even further afield are the *Hopi* (Northern Arizona) and *Papago* (Southern Arizona) tribes. The *Papago* medicine men are known for their breathy croaking and coarse humming,[14] while in the Hopi culture, cooing and hooting in the imitation of owls is heard in lullaby songs.[15]

The Blackfoot tribe of Montana believes singing to be unrelated to speaking. It is the singing sound that is all important: a high tessitura, nasality, falsetto starts, and a pulsing vibrato on long tones--all at a high level of intensity to accommodate singing out of doors and the fact that in Blackfoot pedagogy, high pitches indicate strength and low pitches weakness. The intensity of this tribe's singing has increased over the years, becoming higher and louder, which

---

[11] Carlos Troyer, *Indian Music Lecture: The Zuni Indians and their Music* (Philadelphia: Theodore Presser, 1913).

[12] Louis W. Ballard, *The American Indian Sings*. (Santa Fe: New Southwest Music Publications, 1976).

[13] Tom Bahti, *Southwestern Indian Ceremonials* (Las Vegas: K.C. Publications, 1970/1982).

[14] Ruth Murray Underhill, *Singing for Power, The Song Magic of the Papago Indians of Southern Arizona* (Los Angeles: University of California Press, 1968).

[15] George List, "Song in Hopi Culture, Past and Present." *Journal of International Folk Music Council* 14 (1962): 30-35.

Nettl suggests may be the result of the need to exaggerate their Indian identity as an antidote to the invasion of white culture.[16] In contrast, Arthur Nevin describes the tones of the chants of their sweat-lodge songs as low, "being uttered through the nostrils and mostly monotones."[17] Blackfoot women are known to use a great deal of ornamentation and much less vocal tension than the men; however, there are some women who take on the responsibilities and social status of men and engage in musical behavior more like that of men-- the so called "manly-hearted women." These singers never play to the audience or to one another, but look down during a ceremony.

An ability to project is the most prized quality in a voice among the Omaha tribe (Nebraska). Baritones and mezzo-sopranos are the most common voice types. All sustained tones require the use of vibrato (or tremolo), and vibrato is also used as an expressive device in text painting. For example, in a song of thanksgiving for receiving a horse, the singer will cause his voice to pulsate as if he were singing while riding. In love songs, pulsations are made by bringing the hand to and from the mouth while singing.[18] There are times when Omaha Natives sing and cry simultaneously, such as in a young man's vision quest song that occurs while he wanders in the woods for days without food in order to prepare him for success in life.

Weeping and singing go hand in hand among the singers of the *Yurok* tribe in Northwestern California as well. Here vocal and facial tension, slurring, glottal attacks, nasality, glissando, and tremolo characterize the technique. Singers allow the tone to be affected by the emotional content of a song, rather than striving for absolute precision in pitch or rhythm. This style is especially evident in their Love Medicine songs.[19] There are marked differences between the vocal approaches of

---

[16] Bruno Nettl, *Blackfoot Musical Thought*. (Kent: Kent State University Press, 1989)
[17] Arthur Nevin, "Of the Chants of the Sweat Lodge Songs of the Black Feet Indians in Montana," *The Etude* (October 1920).
[18] Alice C. Fletcher, *A Study of Omaha Indian Music* (Lincoln: University of Nebraska Press, 1994/1893).
[19] Richard Keeling, *Cry for Luck, Sacred Song and Speech among the Yurok, Hupa, and Karok Indians of Northwestern California* (Los Angeles: University of California Press, 1992).

males and females, with women producing a more lyrical sound and men delivering a tense, glottal tone probably having its origins in the manner the men used their voices to lure and trap wild animals in northern hunting culture. However, in the Flower Dance songs (which celebrate a young girl's entrance into puberty), men sing at a soft dynamic level, utilizing a lighter registration.

Cheyenne singers in South Dakota and Northern Nebraska are noted for a long breath line and the use of vowel migration for the sake of ease in singing, usually from closed to open vowels. They sing with or without vibrato depending on the sentiment of what is being sung. The women in this tribe tend to have a smooth, free vocal aesthetic in contrast to the men whose singing tends to be strident. Though Cheyenne women do not play the drum in ceremonies, the men depend on them as backup singers and also benefit by their role as "prompters" to help them remember the songs. Their high pitched laments or howls (ululations) add an element of energy and excitement to a performance.[20]

Like the *Cheyenne*, the *Teton Sioux* (Dakotas) alter their tone quality according to what is being sung: nasality for love songs, wailing sounds for songs of death, a crooning quality for lullabies, and a reverent, natural tone with little nasality for Ghost Dance songs.[21]

The voices of the Northern Wisconsin and Minnesota *Ojibway* singers are likened to the flute. Nasality exists only in the upper register and the tone becomes harsh only when projection over distance is required; in a closed space the tone remains mellow. An *Ojibway* male averages at least two octaves in full voice, using the falsetto only for war cries.[22] In my observation of *Ojibway* pow wows, many male singers were seen to hold their larynx, pressing slightly on high pitches as a tension relieving device, in addition to much ear cupping to help with

---

[20] Virginia Giglio, *Southern Cheyenne Women's Songs* (Norman: University of Oklahoma Press, 1994).
[21] Louis W. Ballard, *The American Indian Sings* (Santa Fe: New Southwest Music Publications, 1976).
[22] Frederick R. Burton, *American Primitive Music* (Port Washington, NY: Kennikat Press, 1909).

ensemble. "The tone quality of [the] women is nasal in the extreme (formerly they even pinched their nose [when they sang]) . . . . "[23]

With the statement, "Air is life; air is song,"[24] we see that the *Kiowas* of Oklahoma look on the act of breathing as a sacred gift from God.

According to Peter Garcia, singing out every day will keep a voice healthy. But there are other remedies that Native Americans have used for vocal ailments: bitterroot (*lewisia rediviva*), to numb a painful throat for vocal longevity during singing; *osha* (*ligusticum porteri*), used as an expectorant for sore throats and bronchial inflammations; sweet sage, to relieve sore throats or for use as a moistener; inhaling sage and peppermint to open the sinuses; at the onset of vocal illness a "good hot sweat" or sucking on a lemon; and the *doza* plant, for soreness and hoarseness (one chews or boils the root and when obtaining it, one must leave a gift at the spot).[25] In some Native cultures, carrying willow branches is thought to make one sing well, as is rubbing dirt on the throat.[26] In the *Navajo* tradition, legend has it that swallowing a piece of turquoise will maintain the beauty of a young singer's voice.

---

[23] Thomas Vennum, "The Changing Role of Women in Ojibway Music History" in *Women in North American Indian Music: Six Essays,* Richard Keeling, ed. (Bloomington: The Society for Ethnomusicology, 1989), 20.
[24] Luke E. Lassiter, *The Power of Kiowa Song* (Tucson: University of Arizona Press, 1998).
[25] Judith Vander, *Shoshone Ghost Dance Religion*. (Chicago: University of Illinois Press, 1997).
[26] Ibid.

THE MAKING OF NATIVE SONGS

Unlike Western Art songs with their links to established literature and poetry, traditional Native American songs are not considered works of art but are simply part of daily life. Mainly a form of prayer, indigenous song was also an early means of recording Native history through an aural/oral tradition, which relied on the highly developed capacity for memory on the part of the musicians.[27] Countless texts and melodies have been handed down. Many are regarded as personal property and may be given as gifts or traded for other songs or concrete objects. They are not "composed" in the Western musical sense, but "made." According to Cipriano Garcia, the late brother of Peter Garcia of San Juan Pueblo, making a song requires four elements: dedication to the traditions, the tune (which comes first), the words that relate to the ceremony being celebrated, and a keen memory--for the songs are generally not written down.[28]

In Amerindian culture, singers and song creators are one and the same. Some inherit the gift, while others learn by rote from their elders. Like a Western composer, who seeks freedom from distraction in his composing, so do Indians seek isolation in order to create their songs. Among some tribes, for a song to wield great power or magic, it must come from dreams, visions, or other supernatural forces. Songs may spring to life through the act of humming or whistling, inspired by nature or personal events. Once complete, the song generally does not change. Sometimes a tune is altered or adapted to new words. Ceremonial songs are usually made of 4-8 melodic phrases lasting 15-20 minutes.

---

[27] A primitive use of music notation in the form of mnemonics existed among the White River or Wapahani Indians and prayer boards with small figures as a means for remembering the words have been seen among the Ojibways.
Theodore Baker, *On the Music of the North American Indians*. Trans. by Ann Buckley (The Netherlands: Fritz Knuf, 1976).

[28] Danny Lichtenfeld, "Music of San Juan Pueblo." Unpublished masters thesis, (New England Conservatory of Music, 1994).

This length is governed by the choreography, which is repeated in the four cardinal directions. Because of this, each seems never ending, with little cadence or repose, reflecting the ongoing cycle of life. Such repetitiveness imparts a litany-like quality found in Western minimalist compositions.

Before a ceremony in the *Tewa* Pueblo tribes, the village composers are requested to prepare the songs--some old and some newly created. The community of singer/composers, ensuring solidarity within the group, revises new songs.[29] The singers and dancers will rehearse with the composers in the *kiva* (the sacred ritual chamber) where the dance steps are recreated. Ceremonies are the domain of the men, but women may be requested to attend the rehearsals. "If the woman is married, [the musicians] must speak to her in front of her husband . . . If she is not married, the request must be made in front of her father, who usually gives his permission."[30] There are generally several lengthy evenings of rehearsal.

To the Native American, a song's melodic line is far more important than the few words that make up its text. The tunes are derived from simple units of speech, which are elaborated and repeated, but done so without losing their simplicity so that the entire community of singers, dancers, and spectators may participate. Despite the existence of quarter tones and frequent "foreign" pitches throughout many Native songs, there tends to be an innate sense of ordered melodic harmony that revolves around a tonic key. *Chippewa* and *Sioux* melodies favor the minor third, which gives the mournful quality that many associate with Indian music. Theodore Baker further suggests that sad songs are in minor modes and joyful ones in major.[31] The *Navajo Athapaskan* language depends on the pitch level of the voice to give a different meaning to the same word, a trait

---

[29] Maria La Vigna, "Okushare, Music for a Winter Ceremony: the Turtle Dance Songs of San Juan Pueblo," *Selected Reports in Ethnomusicology*: 3, no. 2 (1980): 77-99.
[30] Jill Sweet, *Dances of the Tewa Pueblo Indians*. (Santa Fe: School of American Research Press, 1985).
[31] Baker, *North American Indians*

reflected in their melodies.[32] In the *Hopi* culture the influence of Protestant hymnody is heard with its emphasis on the leading tone, while the Spanish influence is seen in the use of melisma in many southwestern tribal melodies.[33] Historical evidence indicates that Catholic missionaries taught singing and musicianship to the Natives, which undoubtedly helped foster hybrid musical styles. A number of *Cheyenne* (Montana) hymns were published under the auspices of the Mennonite Church and show an obvious mixing of Christian and Native traits.[34]

Native songs are monophonic with rare exceptions. Pueblo melodies begin with low pitched introductions and display higher melodic contours in the body of the song, but always with descending lines. *Navajo* melodies are long and chant-like but contain forceful changes in rhythm and melody, frequent grace notes, and few sustained pitches. In the *Shoshone* culture *portamenti* both to and from pitches occur; likewise, the melodies of the love songs of the Flathead Indians are filled with *glissandi*, which stem from the intensity of the emotion-laden texts that cause the performer to weep while singing.[35] Songs of the Eastern Woodlands tribes remind one of a variety of ethnic music styles, including the Scandinavian and African cultures.

In some southwestern tribes each note of the major scale is associated with a color which in turn denotes a direction or other symbols. The melody of a song is shaped according to this system. Troyer states that in *Zuni* music, "Sounds have colors, and colors originate from solar vibrations."[36] The following chart lists the solfege syllables of the Western major scale and their corresponding color and Native symbols.

---

[32] Bierhorst, *Cry from the Earth*
[33] This is not found in Hopi tribe because of their rejection of the Spanish during the Pueblo uprising in 1680.
George List, "Song in Hopi Culture, Past and Present," *Journal of International Folk Music Council*; 14 (1962): 30-35.
[34] Giglio, *Cheyenne Women's Songs*
[35] Alan P. Meriam, *Ethnomusicology of the Flathead Indians* (New York: Wenner-Gren Foundation for Anthropological Research,1967).
[36] Carlos Troyer, *Indian Music Lecture: The Zuni Indians and their Music* (Philadelphia: Theodore Presser, 1913).

PITCH	COLOR	DIRECTION	REPRESENTATION
Do	Yellow	West	Sun, bear, bluebird (songs of praise and joy)
Re	Green		Tree
Mi	Blue	North (South in some regions)	Sky, water, mountain lion, oriole, female
Fa	Red	South	Fire, life, wildcat, parrot, badger
Sol	Brown		
La	Orange	Sunset	
Ti	Purple		(songs of death, requests, contrition)
N/A	Black	North (in some regions)	Male
N/A	White	East	Wolf, magpie
N/A	N/A	Zenith	Eagle
N/A	N/A	Nadir	Shrew [37]

Meters tend to be irregular in Amerindian songs and the rhythm is frequently a mixture of twos and threes. Changes in tempo or shifts from duple to triple rhythm are signaled by the sound of the singers' drum, which also indicates a change in movement or direction by the dancers, the beginning of a new section, or an emphasis on important words. *Ojibway* songs are fascinating for their frequent use of quintuple meter, possibly stemming from their counting system, which is based on groups of five numerals.[38] Furthermore, the drumbeat in most Native songs rarely coincides with the rhythm of the vocal line.

"Knowledge is what makes sound meaningful; to know a song is to know its meaning..." [39]

 --Theresa Carter, *Kiowa*

Native song texts are made up of words that comprise a single thought and scant imagery, which may or may not be on a lengthy melodic framework. In this

---

[37] Troyer, *Indian Music Lecture*; Sweet, *Dances*.
[35] Burton, *American Primitive Music*..
[39] Lassiter, *The Power of Kiowa Song*.

way they resemble many Western operatic arias that use few words but contain much implied subtext and emotion through textual repetition. The Blackfoot Indians of Montana view "white" music as having too many words and feel that it is too much like talking. "If you want to talk," they say, "why don't you talk?" [40]

Frances Densmore compares Native American texts to Japanese Haiku, [41] as does Kenneth Rexroth when he suggests that Indian song texts "are pure poems of sensibility resembling nothing so much as classical Japanese poetry or Mallarmé and certain other modern French and American poets, notably some of the imagists . . . ." [42] These texts often appear to the Native after a very intense physical/spiritual experience such as a fast, or days of solitude in the woods or desert. They reflect the individual's acute sense of pain, heat, cold, or touch and call to mind the deeply physico-spiritual Canticles of St. Francis of Assisi.[43] Rhymes occur rarely, if at all, and Spinden suggests that through repetition there exist "rhyming thoughts" rather than rhyming sounds.[44] Use of the first person pronoun is rare in these texts so there is no barrier between the narrator and the listener. This contributes to the idea of solidarity mentioned in Chapter 2.

The subjects of Native song texts are wide ranging, encompassing the entire experience of a Native American's life and traditions. Many songs and dances celebrate the seasonal cycle: the fall harvest (especially corn, beans, squash and tobacco); winter hunting; springtime rebirth through planting; and summer rain to sustain crops (especially in the very important Corn Dance). There are texts for curing the sick (recognized as the first organized music therapy), success in war, the regeneration of humanity, the puberty rites of young girls, peyote ceremonies, and salt gathering. There are satirical songs leveled at certain individuals, lullabies, songs dealing with everyday chores, horseback riding, and also references to ancestors, supernatural beings, rainbows, the eagle, the dog

---

[40] Nettl, *Blackfoot Musical Thought*.
[41] Frances Densmore, *The Poetry of Indian Songs* (Albuquerque: University of New Mexico Press, 1939).
[42] Kenneth Rexroth, "On American Indian Songs," *Perspectives USA*: 16 (1956):197-201.
[43] Ibid.
[44] Herbert Joseph Spinden, *Songs of the Tewa* (Santa Fe: Sunstone Press, 1993).

(highly regarded as best friend and protector), and the butterfly (as herald to summer and the pollinator of crops). There are *Ojibway* rice-hulling songs, which are now obsolete because of the advances in modern technology for rice harvesting.

Songs occur during games and story telling (an Indian version of music theater) and during the making and drinking of saguaro cactus liquor among the *Papago* (now *O'otam*) tribe in the desert of Southern Arizona.[45] There are also contemporary war songs which honor Natives who have fought in the American Armed Forces, and in the *Ojibway* Nation there are death songs, sung by the person who is dying, or if he is too feeble, by his friends.

Traditional love songs are not plentiful in most Native American tribes, but one may look to the Hispanic influence for those that exist in the southwestern Pueblos.[46] In the *Hopi* tribe there are texts that revolve around courtship, especially during corn grinding time, when the young boys come and play their drums to spur on the girls in their work.[47]

Sioux Ghost Dance songs (known also as *Naraya* songs) derive from the cult begun in 1889 by Wovoka, a Nevada *Paiute* Indian who sought to restore the Native American tribes to their proper place in the world after their ravagement by the white race. The songs invoke the spirits of deceased Indians, underscoring the belief that all Indians living and dead will be reunited in a new and more perfect earthly existence (a hallmark of the *Shoshone* Ghost Dance style was pounding the feet on the ground to try to waken the dead back to life). [48]

In addition to simple poetry, Native songs contain non word syllables known as *vocables*. Rarely found in the middle of words, these syllables usually begin or end song sections. Musicologists have yet to concur on the reasons for

---

[45] Ruth Murray Underhill, *Singing for Power, The Song Magic of the Papago Indians of Southern Arizona* (Los Angeles: University of California Press, 1968).
[46] Spinden, *Tewa*.
[47] List, *Hopi*.
[48] Vander, *Shoshone*. The Ghost Dance Religion spread to many of the tribes in the Plains and Southwest and lead directly to one of the most tragic conflicts in Native and White relations, the notorious Wounded Knee Massacre in which the United States government tried to suppress the movement.

and origins of these sounds, therefore the explanations are numerous. In her research on *Navajo* songs, Charlotte Frisbie suggests that *vocables* derive from archaic or forgotten words of old songs. These may be used as melody "filler" or as a means of lengthening a vowel within a word.[49] They can be stylized exclamations, imitations of animal cries, or other sounds (such as water turning to steam when it is poured on hot stones during a sweat lodge ceremony).[50] *Vocables* may mirror dance steps or may cue the dancers. They sometimes foreshadow the vowel of the next word in a phrase, accommodate breaths in long phrases, or are used simply as a resting place to gather one's thoughts and recuperate vocally. *Vocables* may also signify a kind of Spirit language, originating in stream-of-consciousness improvisations or in dreams, similar to the Gift of Tongues in some Christian religions. There are tribes that employ these wordless sounds as a disguise to prevent outsiders from understanding Native words. Because of their universality, *vocables* enable singers from different tribes and languages to sing together in a nod to solidarity.

Some songs are made up entirely of *vocables*, such as the wordless lullabies sung by Indian women. In *Cheyenne* lullabies, the meaningless syllables "*ma*" and "*ho*" are considered to be effective in calming infants to sleep and also happen to be similar to the word for God-- "*Ma hi yo.*"[51] Another sound reference to the Almighty comes with the sacred syllables of the *Cherokee* and *Hurons*, "*Yo-he-wa*," remarkably similar to the Hebrew word, *Je-ho-va*.[52]

One may draw a number of comparisons between *vocables* and Western literary or musical devices. Observe the opening or closing phrases of many fairy tales: "Once upon a time," or "they lived happily ever after," or similarly the "fa

---

[49] Charlotte Frisbie, "Vocables in Navajo Ceremonial Music," *Enthnomusicology* ; 24, no. 3 (1980) 347-392.
[50] Leanne Hinton, "Vocables in Havasupai Song," in *Southwestern Indian Ritual Drama* (Prospect Heights: Waveland Press, 1989).
[51] Virginia Giglio, *Southern Cheyenne Women's Songs* (Norman: University of Oklahoma Press, 1994), 62
[52] Baker, *North American Indians*.

la la" and "hey nonny nonny " in Elizabethan verse.[53] There also may be some aural/oral similarities between the Native's use of *vocables* and jazz scat singing or the fact that singers in both of these traditions will use their voices to imitate instruments (in the Native's case, percussion or flute).

Vocables are full of sonic meaning and, as one study suggests, each possesses a different emotional value,[54] serving as a vehicle for vocal expression as in the endless scales of Rossini or the ornamental effects of the *stile rappresentativo* of the Florentine Camerata. A Native singer's use of a sustained vocable always with tremolo or vibrato is remarkably similar to the *gruppo* or *battuta di gola* of the early Baroque.

Accompaniment

Ceremonial Native songs are rarely sung a cappella. Many Native singing ensembles are known as "drums," honoring the all important instrument in Native American culture. The drum is believed to have great power. Its sound can symbolize the beating of a heart or a long-awaited thunderstorm. The drum is said to know all and is treated with great respect and must never be beaten with bare hands. The larger instruments are made from trees such as the cottonwood and covered with animal hides. In some tribes, they are tuned before ceremonials and powwows by warming the drum head in front of a spirit fire made with tobacco and cedar. Some drums are fashioned from hollow half gourds, which are suspended in water and played. Others can be filled with water to affect tuning.

As mentioned earlier, the beat of the drum rarely coincides with the rhythm of the singing, except at the beginning or end of sections. This unique polyrhythmic phenomenon between singing and drumming occurs because Native songs follow the irregular meters of the language, so a singer is not locked into

---

[53] Burton, *American Primitive Music*.
[54] Tony Isaacs, "A Brief Introduction to Plains Indian Singing" (Taos: Indian House, 1990).

rigid units of measure. This results in a fluid sense of pulse. Nevertheless, Indians must always have the external pulse in order to sing.

Other percussion instruments include rattles made from dewclaws, tortoise shells or gourds; sleigh bells on leather waistbands (which help call spirits); and in the Navajo culture, an upside-down basket played with dried strips of the yucca plant. Flutes and flageolets are usually associated with love songs and their tone is said to have power over women. *Ojibway* flutes were constructed to emulate the sound of the voice,[55] and conversely, *Maidu* love songs were sung in the imitation of the flute.[56] In the *Teton Sioux* culture the elk whistle (made from the wood of box elder or ash) was used as a courting call by young men,[57] and the *Shoshone* Ghost Dance religion employed whistles made from eagle bones. Eagle whistles also are used during powwows: when a particular song pleases the crowd, the ceremonial master will "whistle the drum" (the singing ensemble), at which time they must repeat the song in its entirety. In the *Hopi* flute ceremony, reed flutes imitate the sound of locusts to bring summer rain,[58] and reeds hidden in a singer's mouth give the effect of a supernatural cry during certain dances of the *Haida* people in the Northwest coastal area.

Stringed instruments are nearly nonexistent in Native culture; however one made with eight strings known as the *harpon* was discovered among the *Apaches*.[59] Western styled instruments have been incorporated into some native music such as the Hispanic influenced *Matachines* Dance on Christmas Day in the Pueblo culture, which makes use of violin or guitar accompaniment. Guitar or accordion is used in the Chicken Scratch Dance in some areas of Arizona and fiddle music handed down by Scottish trappers of the Hudson Bay Company is a staple in the dances of the Alaskan *Athabascan* Indians.

---

[55] Burton, *American Primitive Music.*
[56] Frances Densmore, *Music of the Maidu Indians of California* (Los Angeles: The Southwest Museum, 1958).
[57] Frances Densmore, *Teton Sioux Music and Culture* (Lincoln: University of Nebraska Press, 1918/1992).
[58] Bahti, *Southwestern Indian Ceremonials.*
[59] Baker, *North American Indians.*

Sometimes song accompaniment is provided by singers' voices, as in the percussive ostinato grunting or drone of the *Yuman* tribe during a soloist's rendition. Ensemble grunting has also been recorded among the *Yurok, Hupa,* and *Karoks* in the northwest culture area.[60] Generally *Shoshone* Ghost Dance songs have no accompaniment, but the voice acts as its own drum with rhythmic pulsing. In more recent times, *Cheyenne* women accompany themselves on the omnichord, a modern Japanese-made instrument.[61]

Native Singers

In the sacred territory of Native American singing, a fine line exists between prayerfulness and sheer enjoyment, because Indians love to sing. If you are a singer, you have achieved a certain status. You are a servant of the community and highly regarded. This was evident at all the ceremonies I attended, including the sixth annual Native Roots and Rhythms festival in Santa Fe. Here Natives and the general public have the opportunity to experience the joy of singing first hand in a concert that features a range of traditional and contemporary indigenous performers. At the August 2000 performance, the first singers were a group of men representing all nineteen Pueblo communities of New Mexico who displayed much the same vocal technique as Peter Garcia's singers in San Juan. In contrast, the next group, called the Rio Grande Singers, displayed a high pitched, forward falsetto (much like the controlled "scream" of a hard rock artist). Their jaws were tense and they held their larynxes high, indicative of the Great Plains style of tribal singing. The lead singer was broad chested and tall.

The program continued with one of the most traditional of the contemporary Native singers, Mary Redhouse, a *Navajo* composer, vocalist, and educator. Mary grew up in a musical family near the southern Arizona *Navajo*

---

[60] Richard Keeling, *Cry for Luck.*
[61] Giglio, *Cheyenne Women's Songs*

reservation. Influenced by John Coltrane, Thelonius Monk, and Miles Davis, she combines jazz with Native chants and birdcall imitations. She demonstrated a high belt technique with lots of nasality and clavicular breathing. She made great use of the whistle register to imitate birdcalls and a sometimes consciously chosen breathy tone. Of her own vocal background, Mary says, "I took some classical voice lessons . . . . A teacher tried to eliminate a certain tone in my voice which he perceived to be rather like steel, something that cuts through. It was a Native tone . . . .I decided I couldn't continue that classical tradition . . .I was kicked out of the school choir . . . . because it was perceived that what I was singing was not really music but screaming and shouting . . . ." [62] She is recorded on Canyon Records Label and is a member of the R. Carlos Nakai Quartet.

Other "Roots and Rhythms" acts ranged from folk singers to contemporary rock in which the vocal styles derived primarily from Western traditions. Mathew Andrae is a *Jicarilla Apache* classically trained at New England Conservatory and Berklee College of Music whose music displays a contemporary rock style. Joanne Shenandoah, acclaimed vocalist, composer, and recording artist since 1990 with over eight CDs is a self-taught musician, who crossed the bridge into classical music in a collaboration with the Syracuse Symphony on *SKY WOMAN*, a symphonic piece on *Iroquois* themes and legends from the book of the same name written by Joanne and her husband. Bill Miller is Wisconsin-born Native from the Stockbridge-Muness reservation, whose music ranges from a gentle country mode to a folk/rock style blended with Native chants and instruments. He was named 1999 Artist of Year by the Native American Music Awards. Jerry Alfred, a *Yukon Crow,* sings in his native *Tuchone* language in a Dylanesque, folk style and Star Nayea is a Detroit-raised contemporary Native rock singer.

Other groups and individuals, some of whom have won or been nominated for Native American Music Awards are Rita Coolidge, Buffy Sainte Marie,

---

[62] Native Roots and Rhythms Sixth Annual Native American Performing Arts Festival Program (Santa Fe: August 19, 2000).

Andrew Vasquez, Medicine Dream, Thunderbird Sisters, Randy Wood of the Northern Cree Singers, Jana, Litefoot, Robert Mirabal, Arigon Starr, Blacklodge Singers, Chief Jim Billie, Eagle Eye Cherry, Eyabay, Indigenous, Mary Youngblood, Primeau & Mike, R. Carlos Nakai, Robbie Robertson, Robert Tree Cody, Wayquay, Shouting Mountain, J.H. Francis/Eagle Feather, Whitetale Singers, and many more. Over 25 categories are now presented in these awards, ranging from Artist of the Year and Group of the Year, to Best Powwow Recording and Best Traditional Recording along with a special Thorpe Award in honor of the late Native athlete, Jim Thorpe.

Some Historic Native Singers of Note

Princess Watahwasso (Bright Star), a *Penobscot* Indian and mezzo-soprano, was born in Bangor, Maine, and educated at Cambridge, Massachusetts. She presented a New York recital at Aeolian Hall in 1919.

Tsianina Redfeather, *Creek* and *Cherokee* Native, born in Eufaula, Oklahoma, was engaged for twelve years as a touring recitalist by "Indianist" composer Charles Wakefield Cadman. She also sang for the troops in World War I.

Francis La Flesche, son of an *Omaha* Chief (Joseph La Flesche) and member of the Indian Bureau at Washington D.C., collaborated closely with ethnomusicologist Alice Fletcher during her research at the end of the nineteenth century.

Tetebahbundung was an *Ojibway* tenor, famous for his warmth, power, and artistic ability.

Other singers include: Dr. Charles A. Eastman, Paul Chilson (*Pawnee* tenor), Edna Wooley (*Sioux*) and wife of Thurlow Lieurance, and more recently, White

Eagle, an operatic tenor who had a brief and successful singing career in the early 1990s before succumbing to AIDS.

WESTERN COMPOSERS AND NATIVE SONG

From the 1880s to about 1925, the "Indianist" movement played a role in the development of American art song. The seeds were planted by the authors James Fenimore Cooper and Henry Wadsworth Longfellow who had turned their attention to Amerindian subjects. Another contributing factor to the movement was the founding of the American Folklore Society whose mission was to collect and preserve Negro and Indian melodies. Antonin Dvorak used Native derived material in his Opus 97 Quintet, composed while he was in Spillville, Iowa.

The following is a list of composers whose vocal works contain or have been influenced by the music of the Native American Indian, along with a list of their works.

Louis Wayne Ballard, b.1931; Quapau/Cherokee, Hunka No-Zhe.
    The American Indian Sings: arrangements of Native Songs
    Cantata: *The God will hear* (1966)

Alberto Bimboni, 1882-1960; Italian-American pianist.
    Winona (opera 1926)

Paul Bliss, 1872-1933; Publisher: Willis.
    The Mound-Builders (Cantata for Chorus and SAB soloists)
    The Feast of the Red Corn (Operetta)

John Lewis Browne, 1864-1933; organist.
    An Indian Dance (two part chorus)

Frederick Russell Burton, 1861-1909; published *American Primitive Music* (Kennikat Press, 1909); some songs contain both English and Ojibway texts.

    Banished

    The Beaver Hunt

    Carousal

    Confession

    Doubt: a Death Song

    The Forest Choir

    Gambling Song

    Her Shadow (collaboration with Cadman)

    Hiawatha's Death Song (also for SATB and piano accompaniment)

    In the Forest

    In the Sugar Camp

    The Lake Sheen (both after Ojibway melodies; also for SATB quartet)

    Lonely

    The Lucky Trapper

    Midnight Tryst, A Song of Elopement

    Morning Tryst

    My Bark Canoe (also for unaccompanied SATB quartet)

    The Naked Bear

    Old Shoes

    Parting

    Red Blanket

    Sleepy Time

    A Song of Absence and Longing (also for unaccompanied SATB quartet)

    Song to the Morning Star

    Waubunosa's Longing

    War Song

    Wedding Song

    Winter

Carl Busch, 1862-1943; Danish conductor; Publisher: Oliver Ditson and H.W. Gray.

>Chibiabos
>Death of Chibiabos
>Gitche Manito
>Greeting of Hiawatha
>Onaway Awake
>Indian Lullaby
>The Last Taschastas
>*The Four Winds* (Cantata)

Charles Wakefield Cadman, 1881-1946; composer, organist, music critic. Familiar with the ethnomusicological work of Alice Fletcher and John Comfort Fillmore, Cadman visited several tribes with Francis La Flesche, including the Omaha in 1909. His opera, *Shanewis* (March 23, 1918), was based on the life of Princess Tsianina Redfeather (also Cadman's lecture-recital partner) and had a Metropolitan Opera production under Giulio Gatti-Casazza. *Shanewis* includes twenty Indian melodies which Cadman and other ethnomusicologists had collected. The opera with its all American cast earned twenty-one curtain calls at its premiere and was highly praised in the press. Like many early arrangers of the Negro Spiritual, Cadman sought to popularize Indigenous American music by what might be termed now as "white-washed" versions that would appeal to the mainstream musical public of his day. His many songs with Indian derived melodic material represent a longtime collaboration with the poet, Nelle Richmond Eberhart, whose poetry gives only a slight nod toward Amerindian sources. In his editions Cadman was careful to include an example of the actual tribal melody arranged, as well as its collector's name. He felt that Indian melodies adapted best to solo vocal arrangements or to orchestral treatment, rather than to four-part choral arrangements or piano transcriptions, which were popular at the time. Such operatic artists as Lillian Nordica and Frances Alda programmed his songs. Publisher: Edwin H. Morris, White-Smith.

>From the Long Room of the Sea (Eberhart)

Full Moon, cycle for four solo voices

He who Moves in the Dew (Eberhart)

Her Shadow (collaboration with Burton) and Canoe Song (from *Shanewis*)

Ho, Ye Warriors on the Warpath (Eberhart)

I Found Him on the Mesa (Eberhart)

Music of the American Indian (compilation of nine songs)

The New Trail (Eberhart) mezzo-soprano/baritone duet

Place of Breaking Light (Eberhart)

Spring Song of the Robin Woman (from *Shanewis*)

The Thunderbirds Come from the Cedars (Eberhart)

The Doe-Skin Blanket (Cecil Fanning)

Four American Indian Songs (cycle; also for men's or women's voices)

>From the Land of the Sky-Blue Water (Omaha melody)

The White Dawn is Stealing (Iroquois Melody)

Far Off I Hear a Lover's Flute (Omaha Melody)

The Moon Drops Low (Omaha Melody)

From Wigwam and Tepee (cycle of four songs)

The Warrior Departs (Sop, Bar duet)

Operas:

Daoma or *The Land of Misty Water* (1912)

Ramala, The Land of Misty Water: An Indian Idyll (Eberhart, La Flesche 1909)

Shanewis (1918)

The Sunset Trail (1922)

Operetta:

Lelawala or *The Maid of Niagara* (operetta for mixed chorus)

South in Sonora (Roos)

Cantata:
> *By the Skeena River* for unison chorus (Eberhart)
>
> *Call of the River* (SATB)
>
> *Desert Quest*
>
> *The Far Horizon* (Roos)
>
> *The Father of Waters*
>
> *Indian Love Charm*

John Alden Carpenter, 1876-1951.
> Young Man, Chieftain! (An Indian Prayer)

Samuel Coleridge-Taylor, 1875-1912; Publisher: H.W. Gray and Novello.
> Onaway! Awake, Beloved! (aria from *Hiawatha*)
>
> *Hiawatha* (Cantata)
>> -Hiawatha's Wedding Feast
>>
>> -The Death of Minnehaha
>>
>> -Hiawatha's Departure

Natalie Curtis, 1875-1921; Curtis worked among the Hopis and Zunis and published *The Indian Book* (1907); Publisher: G. Schirmer.
> *Songs of Ancient America*
>
> Three Pueblo Indian Corn-grinding songs
>
> Victory Song (for chorus and mixed voices based on Pawnee Melody)

Brent Michael Davids, current contemporary Mohican composer, published by Earthsongs and Blue Butterfly Group, Tempe, Arizona; many vocal works.
> Mohican Soup (for SATB and two skin drums.1997)
>
> *Native American Suite* (for SATB, percussion and crystal flute, 1995, commissioned by Dale Warland Singers)
>> -Lenape Song (Delaware)

-"49" song, I still love you yet (Apache)

-Zuni Sunrise Song (Pueblo)

Arthur Farwell, 1872-1952; A student of George Chadwick, Farwell was born in St. Paul, Minnesota. He was influenced by ethnomusicologist Alice Fletcher's transcriptions of Amerindian melodies, and also did his own field research. He established a publishing company that he named the Wa-Wan Press (Wa-Wan, from the Omaha meaning, "to sing to someone;" also an intertribal peace ceremony). Wa-Wan's publications came out periodically until 1911 and have since been reprinted by Arno Press (1970). Farwell regarded Indian melodies with respect and considered them as the Native did--a spiritual form of communication connected with religion and ceremony. He joined the Natives in railing against his own society's lust for wealth and power. [63]

Three Indian Songs Op 32 (from Omaha Tribal melodies)
Song of the Deathless Voice
Inketunga's Thunder Song
The Old Man's Love Song (also for mixed chorus)

John Comfort Fillmore, 1843-98; a faculty member at Milwaukee School of Music. He studied at Oberlin and in Leipzig and harmonized the melodies collected by Alice Fletcher at the end of the nineteenth century in *Indian Story and Song from North America* (1900). In so doing, he would have the Natives listen to his harmonizations to attain their approval. Numerous arrangements in original languages, too many to list here.

Anthony Philip Heinrich, 1781-1861; Bohemian émigré, one of the earliest to arrange Native songs.

The Sons of the Woods, an Indian war song

---

[63] Carole Kimball, *Song, A Guide to Style and Literature* (Seattle: PST, Inc., 1996).

Victor Herbert, 1859-1924.
>Opera *Natoma*, (1911)

Frederick Jacobi, 1891-1952; influenced by Pueblo Indian music during the 1920s.
>Tesuque and Tuari, (for string quartet and voice; unpublished, dedicated to Madame Eva Gautier)

Edward F. Johnston, b. 1879-?; Publisher: J. Fischer.
>*Pocohontas* (operetta with Frederick Edmonds, librettist)

Eastwood Lane, 1879-1951; American impressionist.

William Lester, 1889-1956; Publisher: Carl Fischer, Oliver Ditson.
>*Se'a'wan'a*, (The Cherry Maid; Indian Lyric Drama for women's voices Op. 73)
>Trail to the Shadow Land

Thurlow Lieurance, 1880-1963; trained at Cincinnati Conservatory and was employed by the US Government to record Native melodies on the Crow Reservation; Publisher: Theodore Presser.
>Aooah--Love Song from the Red Willow Pueblos (also mixed voices or four-part women's)
>At the foot of the Mound #1, #2 (sop, flute ad lib)
>At the Sundown
>By the Waters of Minnetonka (J.M. Cavanass violin and flute ad lib; also for mixed voices)
>By the Weeping Waters
>Canoe Song (Medicine Moon; with flute)
>A Crow Maiden's Prayer Song

Dying Moon Flower

From an Indian Village (Grinnel's Blackfoot Tales)

From Ghost Dance Canyon

Ghost Pipes (Charles Roos; unpublished)

Her Blanket (from the Navajo)

Hymn to the Sun God

In Mirrored Waters (in Sioux and English; flute and violin ad lib)

Indian Spring Bird--Ski-bi-bi-la (Alfred Fletcher)

Indian Spring Song (for three-part women's voices)

The Lone Loon's Cry (Juanita Roos)

A Lone Owl is calling

Love Song from the Red Willow Pueblos (Edna Dean Proctor)

Lullaby (also for mixed voices)

A Mountain Madrigal--From the Yellow Stone

My Flute Call Haunts the Wild Wood (Charles Roos)

My Lark, My Love (also for mixed voices)

My Silver-throated Fawn--Sioux Love Song (Karl Jones; also two-part women's chorus)

Nine Indian Songs (collection)

Songs of the North American Indians (collection)

O'er the Indian Cradle

The Owl's Bleak Cry

Pakoble--The Rose (Karl Jones; also three-part women's chorus)

Pa-Pup-Ooh--Deer Flower

Pueblo Spring Song

Rainbow Land (violin and cello ad lib)

The Red Birds Sing O'er the Crystal Spring (sop, flute ad lib)

A Rose on an Indian Grave

Rue, A Pueblo Love Song (Alfred Fletcher; violin or flute obl.)

The Sacrifice

A Sioux Serenade (flute ad lib)
The Spirit of Wana
The Swallows (Juanita Roos)
Under the Northern Skies, three songs
The Weaver, The Blanket-Her Rosary
Where Drowsy Waters Steal (Roos)
Where the Papoose Swings
Winnebago Lament
Wounded Fawn

Frederick Knight Logan, 1871-1928; composer of "Missouri Waltz," Publisher: Forster.
Pale Moon (also for voice and orchestra)

Harvey Worthington Loomis, 1865-1930; NY student of Dvorak; Publisher: Oliver Ditson.
Laughing Water
Little Papoose
The Scalp Dance

John W. Metcalf, arranger and composer; Publisher: Arthur Schmidt.
Jibiwanisi

Arthur Nevin, 1871-1943; brother of Ethelbert Nevin, trained at New England Conservatory and influenced by the melodies of the Blackfeet Indians in Montana; Publisher: White-Smith.
Indian Lullaby
Poia (opera 1909)
Twilight, (opera)
A Daughter of the Forest (opera, Chicago,1918)

Partch, Harry, 1901-1974; influenced by Native American music.

Portnoff, Mischa, pianist, composer, arranger on Broadway.
>Song Cycle (1946)
>Her Scarlet Lips are Silent
>Muckwa, the Bear
>Transcriptions of Cadman songs for piano.

Puccini, Giacomo, 1858-1924. In an attempt to utilize an original piece of "Americana" to add color to his opera, *La Fanciulla del West,* Puccini used a Zuni melody, the "Chorus of Virgin Maidens" from "Festive Sun-Dance of the Zunis." According to Arthur Farwell, the tune was recorded around 1904 by collector/composer, Carlos Troyer. It was transformed by Puccini from a joyful Zuni song into Jake Wallace's nostalgic ballad "Che faranno i vecchi miei" in Act I. [64]

Charles Sanford Skilton, 1868-1941; influenced by Native Singing during his tenure at the University of Kansas.
>Kalopin (opera, 1927)
>The Sun Bride (one act opera w/chamber orchestra; radio premiere, 1930)

Karlheinz Stockhausen, b. 1928.
>*In the Sky I am Walking*
>>12 poems from the Chippewa, Teton Sioux, Nootka, Aztec, Ayacucho and Pawnee tribes.

Carlos Troyer, 1837-1920; Protégé of Liszt, Troyer studied the Zuni melodies in the Southwest. His songs were sung by Ernestine Schumann-Heink and David

---

[64] Allan W Atlas, "Belasco and Puccini: 'Old Dog Tray' and the Zuni Indians." *Musical Quarterly* 75, no. 3 (1991): 362-398.

Bispham. They are characterized by simple harmonies, which allowed the melodies to remain prominent. Publisher: Theodore Presser.

Traditional Songs of the Zuni Indians
- Apache Medicine Chant
- Coming of Montezuma
- The Festive Sun Dance of the Zunis
- The Great Rain Dance of the Zunis
- Hunting Song of the Cliff-Dwellers
- Hymn to the Sun
- Incantation upon a Sleeping Infant
- Indian Fire-drill Song "Ura Cura"
- Invocation to the Sun-God
- Lover's Wooing or Blanket Song
- Midnight Visit to the Sacred Shrine
- The Sunrise Call or Echo Song
- Sunset Song

Bessie M Whiteley, *Hiawatha's Childhood* (operetta); Publisher: C.C. Birchard.

Zamecnik, John Stepan, 1872-1953; composer of film music
- Indian Dawn (Charles O. Roos)

APPENDIX A

Song Collectors and Ethnologists

Theodore Baker, ca.1880s

Franz Boas, 1858-1942

Frances Densmore, 1867-1957

Jesse Walter Fewkes, 1850-1930

Alice C. Fletcher, 1838-1923

Benjamin Ives Gilman

George Bird Grinnell, 1849-1938

Francis La Flesche, 1857-1932 (Omaha Indian; collaborated with Alice Fletcher)

Walter McClintock, 1870-1949

James Mooney, 1861-1921

Charles O. Roos (poet), member of the office of Indian Affairs along with composer Thurlow Lieurance

Herbert Joseph Spinden, 1879-1967

APPENDIX B

The eight New Mexican Pueblos are Taos, Picuris, San Juan, Santa Clara, San Ildefonso, Nambe, Pojoaque, and Tesuque, all of which are geographically located north of Santa Fe, New Mexico.

TAOS PUEBLO
PO Box 1846
Taos Pueblo, New Mexico 87571
Phone: (505) 758-9593
Fax: (505) 758-8831

SANTA CLARA PUEBLO
PO Box 580
Espanola, New Mexico 87532
Phone: (505) 753-7330
Fax: (505) 753-8988

PICURIS PUEBLO
PO Box 127
Penasco, New Mexico 87553
Phone: (505) 587-2519
Fax: (505) 587-1071

POJOAQUE PUEBLO
Rt. 11 Box 71
Santa Fe, New Mexico 87501
Phone: (505) 455-2278/2054
Fax: (505) 455-3363/2950

SAN JUAN PUEBLO
PO Box 1099
San Juan, New Mexico
Phone: (505) 852-4400
Fax: (505) 852-4820

NAMBE PUEBLO
Rt. 1 Box 117-BB
Santa Fe, New Mexico 87501
Phone: (505) 455-2036
Fax: (505) 455-2038

SAN ILDEFONSO
Rt. 5 Box 315-A
Santa Fe, New Mexico 87501
Phone: (505) 455-2273
Fax: (505) 455-7351

TESUQUE PUEBLO
Rt. 5 Box 360T
Santa Fe, New Mexico 87501
Phone: (505) 983-2667
Fax: (505) 983-2038

APPENDIX C

Selected Native Web Sites
www.nativeamericanmusic.com
www.canyonrecords.com
www.indianpueblos.org
www.artnewmexico.com/eightnorthern

APPENDIX D

Selected Recordings from San Juan Pueblo

Songs of My People, Peter Garcia and the Garcia Brothers, CDT-133
Music of the World, Ltd.
P.O. Box 3620
Chapel Hill, NC 27515-3620

Deer Dance Songs of San Juan Pueblo, IH-1103
Indian House
Box 472
Taos, NM 87571

The Tewa Indian Women's Choir, Fun and Social Song from San Juan, TWC-2
Tewa Indian Women's Choir
P.O. Box 27
San Juan Pueblo, NM 87566

Turtle Dance Songs of the San Juan Pueblo, IH-1001
Indian House
Box 472
Taos, NM 87571

Cloud Dance Songs of the San Juan Pueblo, IH-1102
Indian House
Box 472
Taos, NM 87571

BIBLIOGRAPHY

Atlas, Allan W. "Belasco and Puccini: 'Old Dog Tray' and the Zuni Indians," *Musical Quarterly*; 75, no. 3 (1991): 362-398.

Bahti, Tom. *Southwestern Indian Ceremonials*. Las Vegas: K.C. Publications, 1970/1982.

Baker, Theodore. *On the Music of the North American Indians*. Trans. by Ann Buckley. The Netherlands: Fritz Knuf, 1976.

Ballard, Louis W. *The American Indian Sings*. Santa Fe: New Southwest Music Publications, 1976.

Bierhorst, John. *A Cry from the Earth, Music of the North American Indians*. Santa Fe: Ancient City Press, 1979.

Bierhorst, John. *A Cry from the Earth, Music of the North American Indians*. Washington: Folkways/Smithsonian CD F-37777, 1979.

Braine, Susan. *Drumbeat, Heartbeat, A Celebration of the Powwow*. Minneapolis: Lerner Publications,1995.

Burton, Frederick R. *American Primitive Music*. Port Washington, NY: Kennikat Press, 1909.

Chase, Gilbert. "The Indianist Movement in American Music." New York: New World Records LP NW 213, 1977.

Creation's Journey. Native American Music. Washington, D.C.: Smithsonian/ Folkways Recordings. CD SF 40410, 1994.

Curtis, Natalie. *The Indians' Book*. New York: Harper and Brothers, 1907.

Densmore, Frances. "Recent Developments in the Study of Indian Music." *The Etude (*October 1920).

_____ *The Poetry of Indian Songs*. Albuquerque: University of New Mexico Press, 1939.

_____ *Music of the Maidu Indians of California.* Los Angeles: The Southwest Museum, 1958.

_____ *Teton Sioux Music and Culture.* Lincoln: University of Nebraska Press, 1918/1992.

The Etude. "Music of the American Indian." (October 1920).

Farwell, Arthur. *American Indian Melodies.* Newton Center, MA: Wa-Wan Press, 1901.

Fletcher, Alice C. *A Study of Omaha Indian Music.* Lincoln: University of Nebraska Press, 1994/1893.

_____ *Indian Games and Dances with Native Songs.* Lincoln: University of Nebraska Press, 1994.

Frisbie, Charlotee "Vocables in Navajo Ceremonial Music." *Enthnomusicology*; 24, no. 3 (1980): 347-392.

Garcia, Peter. Interview by the author. San Juan Pueblo, NM: Tape recording, September 18, 2000.

_____ "Perspectives of a Contemporary Tewa Composer" in *Musical Repercussions of 1492* (1992) 93-96.

Giglio, Virginia. *Southern Cheyenne Women's Songs.* Norman: University of Oklahoma Press, 1994.

Goodman, Linda J. "The Form and Function of the Basket Dance of San Juan Pueblo." Unpublished masters thesis, Wesleyan University, 1968.

_____ "Native American Performance Series: Pueblo and Navajo Music." Program notes, 1988.

Heidsiek, Ralph. *Music of the Luiseño Indians of Southern California.* Los Angeles: University of California, 1966.

Heth, Charlotte. *Native American Dances: Ceremonies and Social Traditions.* Washington DC: National Museum of the American Indian, Smithsonian Institution, with Fulcrum Publishing, 1993.

_____ "The Traditional Music of North American Indians." *Selected Reports in Ethnomusicology*, 3, no. 2 (1980).

Hinton, Leanne. "Vocables in Havasupai Song" in *Southwestern Indian Ritual Drama.* Prospect Heights: Waveland Press, 1989.

Isaacs, Tony. "A Brief Introduction to Plains Indian Singing." Taos: Indian House, 1990.

Keeling, Richard. *Cry for Luck, Sacred Song and Speech among the Yurok, Hupa, and Karok Indians of Northwestern California.* Los Angeles: University of California Press, 1992.

Kimball, Carole. *Song, A Guide to Style and Literature.* Seattle: PST. . . , Inc., 1996.

Kurath, Gertrude. *Music and Dance of the Tewa Pueblos.* Santa Fe: Museum of New Mexico Press, 1970.

La Vigna, Maria. "Okushare, Music for a Winter Ceremony: the Turtle Dance Songs of San Juan Pueblo." *Selected Reports in Ethnomusicology*: 3, no. 2 (1980): 77-99.

Lassiter, Luke E. *The Power of Kiowa Song.* Tucson: University of Arizona Press, 1998.

Lichtenfeld, Danny. "Music of San Juan Pueblo." Unpublished masters thesis, New England Conservatory of Music, 1994.

Lieurance, Thurlow. "The Musical Soul of the American Indian." *The Etude,* (October 1920): 655

List, George. "Song in Hopi Culture, Past and Present." *Journal of International Folk Music Council*; 14 (1962):30-35.

_____ "Hopi Kachina Dance Songs." *Ethnomusicology*; 41, no. 3 (1997): 413-432.

Meriam, Alan P. *Ethnomusicology of the Flathead Indians.* New York: Wenner-Gren Foundation for Anthropological Research, 1967.

Native American Traditions. CD SF 40408, Washington D.C.: Smithsonian/ Folkways Recordings, 1992.

Native Roots and Rhythms Sixth Annual Native American Performing Arts Festival Program. Santa Fe: Aug 19, 2000.

Nettl, Bruno. *Blackfoot Musical Thought*. Kent: Kent State University Press, 1989.

Nevin, Arthur. "Of the Chants of the Sweat Lodge Songs of the Black Feet Indians in Montana." *The Etude* (October 1920).

Ortiz, Alfonso. *The Tewa World: Space, Time, Being and Becoming a Pueblo Society*. Chicago: University of Chicago Press, 1969.

Portnoff, Mischa. *The American Indian in Song*. New York: Edwin H. Morris, 1968.

Powers, William K. "Ogalala Song Terminology." *Selected Reports in Ethnomusicology* 3, no. 2 (1977): 23-41.

Rexroth, Kenneth. "On American Indian Songs." *Perspectives USA*: 16 (1956):197-201..

Rhodes, Willard. "North American Indian Music: a bibliographic survey of anthropological theory." *Music Library Association Notes*: 10 (1952):33-45.

Ross, Danita "Musical Mission: Taos studio keeps tribal songs on the record." *New Mexico Magazine*; 70, no. 8 (1992): 39-44..

Spinden, Herbert Joseph. *Songs of the Tewa*. Santa Fe: Sunstone Press, 1993.

Sweet, Jill. *Dances of the Tewa Pueblo Indians*. Santa Fe: School of American Research Press, 1985.

Tawa, Nicholas. Liner Notes. *An Old Song Resung*. CD 80463-2 New York: New World Records, 1977/1995.

Tedlock, Barbara. "Songs of the Zuni Kachina Society." *Southwestern Indian Ritual Drama* Albuquerque: University of New Mexico Press, 1980.

Troyer, Carlos. "The Zuni Indians and their Music." Philadelphia: Theodore Presser, 1913.

Turner, Geoffrey. *Indians of North America*. New York: Sterling Publishing Co., Inc., 1992.

Navajo Creation Chants. Liner notes from Recording. Peabody Museum of Harvard University

Underhill, Ruth Murray. *Singing for Power, The Song Magic of the Papago Indians of Southern Arizona*. Los Angeles: University of California Press, 1968.

Vander, Judith. *Shoshone Ghost Dance Religion*. Chicago: University of Illinois Press, 1997.

Vennum, Thomas. "The Changing Role of Women in Ojibway Music History." in *Women in North American Indian Music: Six Essays.* Richard Keeling, ed. Bloomington: The Society for Ethnomusicology, 1989.

Villamil, Victoria. *A Singer's Guide to the American Art Song 1870-1980*. Metuchen: Scarecrow, 1993.

Waldman, Carl. Atlas of the North American Indian. New York: Facts on File, Inc.,1985.

Weinman, Janice. "The Influence of Pueblo Worldview on the Construction of its Vocal Music." *Ethnomusicology*, 14, no. 2 (1970): 313-315.

Wisconsin Powow/Naamikaaged: Dancer for the People. Video recording, SF 48004. Washington DC: Smithsonian Institution, 1996.

Yeh, Nora, "The Pogonshare Ceremony of the Tewa, San Juan, NM." *Selected Reports in Ethnomusicology*; 3, no. 2: 101-145.

INDEX

A
African culture, 25
Alfred, Jerry, 33
American Folklore Society, 37
Andrae, Mathew, 33
animals, 26
Apache tribe, 31, 33, 42, 47
Athabascan tribe, 31

B
Billie, Chief Jim, 34
Blackfoot tribe, 18, 19, 27, 44, 45
Blacklodge Singers, 34
Bright Star, 34

C
Cadman, Charles Wakefield, 34, 39-41
Catholicism/Christianity, 1, 6, 10-12, 25, 29
Cherokee tribe, 29, 34, 37
Cheyenne tribe, 16, 20, 25, 29, 32
children, 5
Chilson, Paul, 34
Chippewa tribe, 24, 46
Cody, Robert Tree, 34
colors, 6, 26
Coolidge, Rita, 33
Cooper, James Fenimore, 37
corn, 2, 5, 12, 27, 28, 41
costume and dress, 2
Creek tribe, 34
Crow tribe, 33, 34

D
dances
    Buffalo, 5
    Butterfly, 5
    Chicken scratch, 31
    Cloud, 12, 51
    Eagle, 5
    Flower, 20
    Ghost, 20, 28, 31, 32, 44
    Harvest, 1, 2, 3, 7, 27, 28
    Matachines, 10, 11, 31
    preparation of, 4, 5
    steps, 10
    Sunset, 11
    Tembishare, 1, 2, 3
    Turtle, 5, 7, 10, 11, 51
    Winter Curing, 18
    Yeibichai, 18
Davids, Brent Michael, 41
drum, 2, 4, 5, 7, 9-12, 20, 26, 28, 30-32
Dvorak, Antonin, 37, 45

E
Eagle Eye Cherry, 34
Eagle Feather, J.H. Francis, 34
Eastern Woodlands tribe, 25
Eastman, Dr. Charles A., 34
elements (the), 5-6, 27
Eyabay, 34

F
Farwell, Arthur, 42, 46
Fillmore, John Comfort, 39, 42
Flathead tribe, 25

G
Garcia family, 1-3, 13, 17, 21, 23, 32, 50

H
Haida tribe, 31
Hopi tribe, 18, 25, 28, 31, 41
Hudson Bay Company, 31
Hupa tribe, 32
Huron tribe, 29

I
Indianist movement, 34, 37

Indigenous, 34
instruments
    accordion, 6, 31
    baskets, 31
    bells, 31
    drum, 2, 4, 5, 7, 9-12, 20, 26, 28, 30-32
    flute, 19, 20, 30, 31, 40, 41, 43-45
    guitar, 5-6, 10, 31
    harpon, 31
    omnichord, 32
    reeds, 31
    rattle, 5, 31
    violin, 10, 31, 43-44
    whistles, 31
Iroquois tribe, 33, 40

J
Japanese culture, 27, 32
Jana, 32

K
kachina, 5, 12
Karok tribe, 32
Kiowa tribe, 21, 26
kiva, 6, 24
koshares, 2, 12

L
La Flesche, Francis, 34, 39, 40, 48
La Flesche, Joseph, 34
Language, 4, 11, 15, 17, 24, 29, 30, 33
Lieurance, Thurlow, 34, 43, 48
Litefoot, 34
Longfellow, Henry Wadsworth, 37

M
Maidu tribe, 31
Medicine Dream, 34
memory, 16, 23
Mennonite, 25
Miller, Bill, 33
Minimalism, 24

Mirabal, Robert, 34
Mohican tribe, 41

N
Nakai, R. Carlos, 33, 34
Native American Music Awards, 33
Native Roots and Rhythm Festival, 34
Navajo tribe, 18, 21, 24, 25, 29, 31, 32, 44
Nayea, Star, 33
Nevin, Arthur, 45
Northern Cree Singers, 34

O
Ojibway tribe, 20, 23, 26, 28, 31, 34, 38
Ogalala tribe, 15
Omaha tribe, 19, 34, 39, 40, 42, 48
O'otam tribe, 28

P
Papago tribe, 18, 28
Paiute tribe, 28
Pawnee tribe, 34, 41, 46
Pedagogy
    Similarities to Western, 16-17
Penobscot tribe, 34
Plains Indians, 11, 17, 28, 32
prayer, 23
Primeau and Mike, 34
Protestant, 25
Puccini, Giacomo, 46
pueblos, 11, 12, 17, 18, 24, 25, 28, 31, 32, 41-44, 49
    Laguna, 13, 49
    Nambe, 49
    Picuris, 49
    Pojoaque, 14
    San Ildefonso, 49
    San Juan, 1, 3, 10, 17, 23, 32, 49-51
    Santa Clara, 49
    Taos, 49

R
Redfeather, Tsianina, 34, 39
Redhouse, Mary, 32
religions, non-native, 1, 6, 10-12, 25, 29
Rio Grande Singers, 32
Robertson, Robbie, 34

S
Sainte Marie, Buffy, 33
Santa Fe, 1, 32, 49
Scandinavian culture, 25
Shenandoah, Joanne, 33
Shoshone tribe, 25, 28, 31, 32
Shouting Mountain, 34
singers, 32-35
Sioux tribe, 20, 24, 28, 31, 34, 44-46
Sky Woman, 33
songs
    art songs, 23, 37
    composition of, 4, 22-26
    contemporary folk and rock, 32-34
    glissando, 19, 25
    hapimbe, 12
    harmony, 24
    hymnody, 24
    jazz, and, 30, 33
    leading tone, 25
    melody, 6, 25, 29, 39
    melisma, 25
    meter and rhythm, 4, 10, 17, 19, 25, 26, 30, 32
    monophony, 25
    notation, 4, 23
    pitch representation, 26
    portamento, 25
    polyrhythm, 30
    pueblo melody, 25
    quarter tones, 24
    rhythm, 4, 10, 17, 19, 25, 26, 30, 32
    similarities to western compositions, 23-25, 27, 29, 31, 33
    Spanish influence, 1, 11, 25, 28, 31
    structure, 23-24
    tempo, 9, 26
song texts, 16, 23, 25, 26-28
    animals, 26
    clarity, 2, 7
    comparisons to other poetic styles, 23, 25, 27-30
    painting, 19
    rhymes, 27
    similarities to Western texts, 27-30
    subjects, 27-28
song types
    American armed forces, 28
    Animals, 26
    death, 20, 26, 28, 38, 39, 41
    Flower Dance songs, 20
    games, 28
    Ghost Dance, 20, 28, 31, 32, 44
    harvest, 1-3, 7, 27, 28
    lullabies, 16, 20, 27, 29, 39, 44, 45
    Love Medicine, 19
    love songs, 19, 20, 25, 28, 31, 40-44, 47
    Naraya, 28
    peyote, 27
    prayer, 23, 41, 43
    puberty rites, 20, 27
    rice hulling, 28
    saguaro cactus liquor, 28
    sweat lodge, 29
    thanksgiving, 19
    war, 28
Starr, Arigon, 34

T
Tetebahbundung,, 34
Tewa, 1-4, 6-8, 10-12, 16, 17, 23, 24
Thorpe, Jim, 31
Thunderbird Sisters, 34
Tuchone language, 33

Tribes, also see Pueblos
    Apaches, 31, 33, 42, 47
    Athabascan, 31
    Blackfoot, 18, 19, 27, 44, 45
    Cherokee, 29, 34, 37
    Cheyenne, 16, 20, 25, 29, 32
    Chippewa, 24, 46
    Creek, 34
    Eastern Woodlands, 25
    Flathead, 25
    Haida, 31
    Hopi, 18, 25, 28, 31, 41
    Hupa, 32
    Hurons, 29
    Iroquois, 33, 40
    Karoks, 32
    Kiowa, 21, 26
    Maidu, 31
    Mohican, 41
    Navajo, 18, 21, 24, 25, 29, 31, 32, 44
    Ojibway, 20, 23, 26, 28, 31, 34, 38
    Ogalala, 15
    Omaha, 19, 34, 39, 40, 42, 48
    O'otam, 28
    Papago, 18, 28
    Paiute, 28
    Pawnee, 34, 41, 46
    Penobscot, 34
    Shoshone, 25, 28, 31, 34, 44-46
    Sioux, 20, 24, 28, 31, 34, 44, 45, 46
    Wapahani, 23
    Yukon Crow, 33
    Yuman, 32
    Yurok, 19, 32
    Zuni, 17, 18, 25, 41, 42, 46, 47
Troyer, Carlos, 18, 25, 46, 47

U
ululations, 16, 20

V
Vasquez, Andrew, 34
vocables, 7, 16, 28-30
    comparisons to Baroque ornamentation, 30
    comparisons to Elizabethan poetic language, 30
    comparisons to Gift of Tongues, 29
    comparisons to Jazz, 30
vocal health, 7-8, 15, 21
    bitterroot, 7, 21
    bronchial inflammations, 21
    dirt, 21
    doza plant, 21
    osa'puh, 7
    osha, 21
    peppermint, 21
    remedys, 8, 21
    sage, 21
    tension relief, 21
    turquoise, 21
vocal technique, 2, 15-17, 33
    anatomy, 17-18
    as accompaniment, 31
    belting, 33
    breathing, 2, 8-10, 16-18, 20, 21, 29, 33
    diction, 6-7,
    dynamics, 6-9, 15, 16, 18, 20
    emotions, 9, 19, 25, 27, 30
    falsetto, 11, 16-18, 20, 32
    glottal stops, 17, 19, 20
    grunting, 32
    larynx, 20, 32
    nasality, 17-21, 33
    parallels to classical western, 15-16
    pedagogical terms, 15
    posture, 2, 9-10, 32
    range, 2, 6, 16-19
    registration, 20, 33
    resonance, 8, 16
    styles, 16-18

    teaching of, 5, 10, 33
    tone, 15, 19-21, 33
    ululations, 16, 20
    vibrato, 18-20, 30

W
Wapahani tribe, 23
Watahwasso, Princess, 34
Wayquay, 34
White Eagle, 34
Whitetale Singers, 34
Wood, Randy, 34
Wooley, Edna, 34
women, 2, 16, 18-21, 24, 26-29, 31, 32, 40, 43, 44, 50
Wovoka, 27, 28

    vowels, 2, 7, 16, 17, 20, 29
        see vocables
    whistle register, 33

X

Y
Yeibichai, 18
Youngblood, Mary, 34
Yukon Crow tribe, 33
Yuman tribe, 32
Yurok tribe, 19, 32

Z
Zuni tribe, 17, 18, 25, 41, 42, 46, 47

NATIVE AMERICAN STUDIES

1. John James Collins, **Native American Religions: A Geographical Survey**
2. Maureen Korp, **The Sacred Geography of the American Mound Builders**
3. Giorgio Mariani, **Post-Tribal Epics: The Native American Novel Between Tradition and Modernity**
4. Mikle Dave Ledgerwood, **Images of the "Indian" in Four New-World Literatures**
5. Laurence Armand French, **The Qualla Cherokee Surviving in Two Worlds**
6. Robert L. Berner, **Defining American Indian Literature: One Nation Divisible**
7. Thomas A. Britten, **A Brief History of the Seminole-Negro Indian Scouts**
8. Guillermo Bartelt, **Socio- and Stylolinguistic Perspectives on American Indian English Texts**
9. Rosemary Lyons, **A Comparison of the Works of Antonine Maillet of the Acadian Tradition of New Brunswick, Canada, and Louise Erdrich of the Ojibwe of North America, with the Poems of Longfellow**
10. Ted Fortier, **Religion and Resistance in the Encounter Between the Coeur d'Alene Indians and Jesuit Missionaries**
11. Gary Lee Sligh, **A Study of Native American Women Novelists–Sophia Alice Callahan, Mourning Dove, and Ella Cara Deloria**
12. Mary Ellen Meredith and Howard Meredith, **Reflection on Cherokee Literary Expression**
13. Susan Forsyth, **Representing the Massacre of American Indians at Wounded Knee, 1890-2000**
14. William Douglas Powers, **An Eliadean Interpretation of Frank G. Speck's Account of the Cherokee Booger Dance**
15. Le Anne E. Silvey, **Ordinal Position and Role Development of the Firstborn American Indian Daughter Within Her Family of Origin**
16. William J. Lavonis, **A Study of Native American Singing and Song**

www.ingramcontent.com/pod-product-compliance
Lightning Source LLC
Chambersburg PA
CBHW021003230426
43666CB00005B/264